Religions of the World

Islam

Rita Faelli

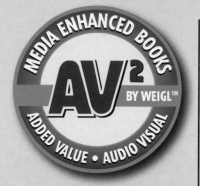

AV² provides enriched content that supplements and complements ... Weigl's AV² books strive to create inspired learning and engage young ... in a total learning experience.

Your AV² Media Enhanced books come alive with...

Audio
Listen to sections of the book read aloud.

Key Words
Study vocabulary, and complete a matching word activity.

Video
Watch informative video clips.

Quizzes
Test your knowledge.

Embedded Weblinks
Gain additional information for research.

Slide Show
View images and captions, and prepare a presentation.

Try This!
Complete activities and hands-on experiments.

... and much, much more!

Go to **www.av2books.com**, and enter this book's unique code.

BOOK CODE

Z264639

AV² by Weigl brings you media enhanced books that support active learning.

Published by AV² by Weigl
350 5th Avenue, 59th Floor
New York, NY 10118
Website: www.av2books.com

Library of Congress Control Number: 2015942087

ISBN 978-1-4896-4035-2 (hardcover)
ISBN 978-1-4896-4036-9 (soft cover)
ISBN 978-1-4896-4037-6 (single user eBook)
ISBN 978-1-4896-4038-3 (multi-user eBook)

Printed in the United States of America in Brainerd, Minnesota
2 3 4 5 6 7 8 9 0 21 20 19 18 17

082017
051917

Photo Credits

The publisher gratefully acknowledges the photo suppliers for this title: iStock, page 1; Getty Images, page 5; Lauri Dammert, page 4; Daniel Tang, page 6; Alison Hausmann, page 24; Wayne Walton, Lonely Planet Images, page 25; Phil Sigin-Lavdanski, page 28. All other photographs and illustrations are © copyright UC Publishing Pty Ltd.

Every reasonable effort has been made to trace ownership and to obtain permission to reprint copyright material. The publishers would be pleased to have any errors or omissions brought to their attention so that they may be corrected in subsequent printings.

First published in 2006 by Blake Publishing
Copyright © 2006 Blake Publishing

Contents

What Is Islam?

Islam is a religion followed by many people around the world. People who follow Islam are called **Muslims**.

Islam began in the Middle East. The language of Muslim worship is **Arabic**.

Word facts

The word Islam and the word Muslim both come from an Arabic word that means submission. For Muslims, this means to accept and obey God.

The Dome of the Rock shrine in Jerusalem is an important holy site to Muslims. It is built where the Prophet Muhammad is believed to have ascended to heaven.

Who Are Muslims?

Over the centuries, Islam spread from the Middle East to different parts of the world, including Asia and Europe. Many Muslims live in these countries.

More recently, Muslims have migrated to countries like Canada, Britain, the United States and Australia. No matter what part of the world Muslims are from, they see themselves as one large family.

Fast fact

The worldwide community of Muslims is called the **Ummah**.

What Do Muslims Believe?

Muslims believe in one God. Muslims call God **Allah**.

They believe that Allah created the universe, the world and everything in it. Muslims only worship Allah. Muslims believe it is their duty to worship Allah because of everything He has provided.

Fast fact

According to Islamic tradition, there are 99 names for Allah. Each of these names describes an aspect of Allah, such as Allah the merciful.

Messengers from God

Muslims believe that Allah sent special people, called **prophets**, to Earth. The prophets are Allah's messengers.

Muslims believe that Allah sent many prophets to teach people how to live good lives. The last prophet Allah sent was called Muhammad.

Fast fact
The Prophet Muhammad's name, written in Arabic script, is common in Islamic art.

The Prophet Muhammad

The Prophet Muhammad was born in Mecca, a town in Saudi Arabia, about 1,400 years ago.

Muslims believe that Allah sent an angel to give Muhammad His messages. These messages were later written down. They became the **Qur'an**, the Muslim holy book. They include the Five Pillars of Islam.

Fast fact

Mecca is the holy city of Islam. Every year, about three million Muslims make a special journey to Mecca. This journey is called a **pilgrimage**.

The Five Pillars of Islam

Muslims have five key duties they try to carry out. These are called the Five Pillars of Islam.

The Five Pillars of Islam are very important as they are the basis of Muslim life.

The **First Pillar** is believing and saying the words: "There is no god but GOD (Allah) and Muhammad is His messenger".

The **Second Pillar** is praying five times a day. Prayers are performed at dawn, midday, late afternoon, sunset and nightfall. The prayers contain verses from the Qur'an.

The **Third Pillar** is giving a certain amount of one's savings to help others, such as the poor.

The **Fourth Pillar** is fasting, which is going without food or drink, from dawn to sunset, every day during the month of Ramadan.

The **Fifth Pillar** is making the journey to Mecca, the holiest of all places for Muslims. Every Muslim who can afford it is expected to make the journey to Mecca once in their lifetime.

What Is the Muslim Holy Book?

Muslims believe that Allah gave clear rules and instructions about how to lead a good life. These instructions are found in the Muslim holy book, the Qur'an.

Muslims believe that the words in the Qur'an are Allah's own words. Therefore, the Qur'an can never be changed.

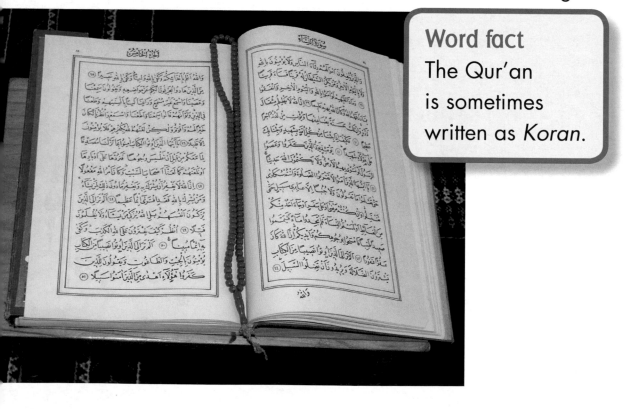

Word fact
The Qur'an is sometimes written as *Koran*.

The Qur'an contains many important messages for Muslims and it is treated with great respect.

Before reading it, Muslims wash very carefully. The Qur'an is never allowed to touch the ground. It is usually placed on a special stool.

Fast fact
The language of the Qur'an is Arabic. However, often people read and study the meanings of the Qur'an in their own language.

Prayers

Praying to Allah is a very important part of Islam. These special prayers are called **Salat**.

The Qur'an tells Muslims how they should pray. Muslims are expected to pray five times a day, no matter what they are doing, or where they happen to be. A special mat is sometimes used for prayers.

When Muslims pray, they face in the direction of the holy city of Mecca.

The prayers have names and are performed at certain times of the day. Mosques have clocks that show the different times these prayers are performed.

The prayers consist of special words and actions. It is important to make the correct movements and say the words correctly.

Where Do Muslims Worship?

Muslims can pray at home or in a special place for worship, called a **mosque**.

Mosques often have a **minaret** which is like a small tower. In some countries, when it is time for prayers, a person calls people to prayer from the minaret.

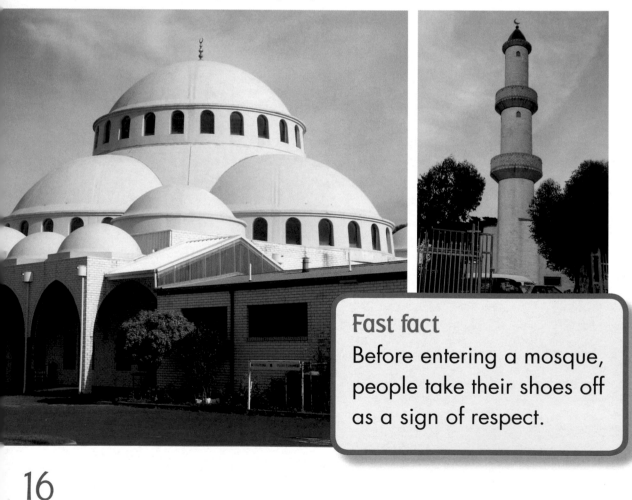

Fast fact
Before entering a mosque, people take their shoes off as a sign of respect.

Inside a Mosque

There are no chairs inside a mosque. People stand, bow, and kneel to worship.

There are separate prayer areas for men and women. On one wall of the mosque, there is special place which shows the direction you face for praying.

Many mosques are beautifully decorated.

The walls and windows may have geometric patterns or flowers on them. The floor is usually covered in beautifully patterned carpet.

Fast fact
There are no statues or paintings of people inside a mosque.

A special form of decoration in Islam is called **calligraphy**. Calligraphy is the art of handwriting.

Most mosques use calligraphy for decoration.

Fast fact

Islamic calligraphy began when people started to write out sections from the Qur'an. They wanted to make the writing beautiful and special, to show how important the words were to them. At first, the words were written on paper. Then people started to decorate tiles and pottery as well.

Wudu

At the mosque, there is also a place where people wash before prayers. This washing before prayers is called **wudu**.

Wudu requires a person to wash different parts of their body in a special way. It is not about being clean or dirty. It is about preparing to pray before Allah.

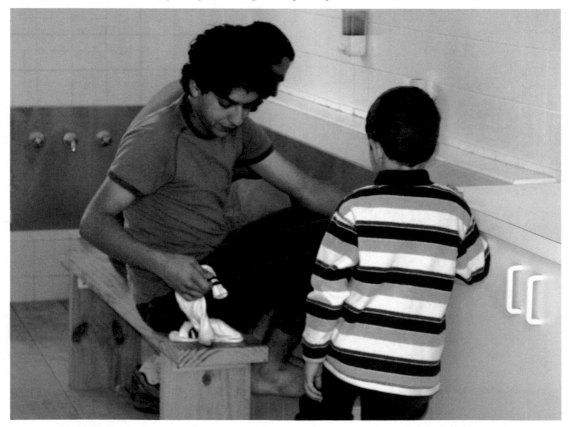

The Imam

The work of an **imam** is to lead the five daily prayers at the mosque. He also gives short talks or sermons before the Friday prayers.

The imam also leads prayers and reads sermons at special occasions, such as marriages or funerals. Because an imam has studied Islam and the Qur'an, he helps other Muslims learn more about their religion.

Rules about Food

The Qur'an tells Muslims what food they can eat and what food is not permitted.

Food that Muslims are allowed to eat is called **halal**. This means permitted. Food which they cannot eat is **haram**. This means forbidden.

Muslims can eat most things but anything that comes from a pig is forbidden.

Clothing

Islam teaches that it is important to be modest and respectful. This also applies to the way men and women dress.

Islam teaches that showing off your body is wrong. In Islam, men should at least be covered from the waist to the knees. Some Muslim women wear a **hijab**. A hijab is a scarf or veil. Some women also wear a loose-fitting, full-length dress.

Life Events

Birth

When a Muslim baby is born, it is welcomed into the family of Islam. This is done by making sure that the first word that the baby hears is Allah.

Marriage

Muslim marriage ceremonies are often held at home. The man and woman exchange vows in front of witnesses. The marriage is then blessed by readings from the Qur'an.

Fast fact

It is traditional for Arab Muslim brides to paint beautiful patterns on their hands and feet. For this they use **henna**, a paste from the henna plant. It stains the skin a dark red color.

Death

When a Muslim dies, the funeral is a simple event. The body is buried as soon as possible, usually within 24 hours of death.

After death, the body is washed and then wrapped in layers of white cloth. Often the body is taken to a mosque and the imam, or someone who was close to the deceased, says the funeral prayer.

Muslims place the body into the ground. The face of the body is turned so that it is facing the direction of the holy city of Mecca.

Learning about Islam

Muslim children begin to learn about Islam when they are very young. Their parents teach them the basics about their religion.

They learn how to recite the Qur'an, how to memorise short passages from it, the proper way to pray, and how a Muslim should behave.

Fast fact

Some Muslim children go to weekend school to learn about Islam. The weekend school is usually held at the local mosque. Children learn to read from the Qur'an and they may also study the language of their parents.

Some Muslim children attend private schools where the Qur'an is taught.

Students at these schools learn the same subjects as taught in public schools but they also learn about Islam.

Ramadan and Eid al-Fitr

Ramadan is the ninth month of the Muslim calendar and is called the holy month. The end of Ramadan is celebrated with a festival called **Eid al-Fitr**.

Ramadan is an important time for Muslims all over the world. They believe that the Prophet Muhammad received Allah's message during Ramadan.

Adult Muslims are expected to fast during daylight hours during Ramadan. They eat a light meal before dawn, then go without food or drink all day until sunset.

Before the Eid festival, everyone gives money to charity and there are special prayers held at the mosque. Muslim families gather and give each other gifts. Sometimes a special fair is held for the community. Everyone is welcome.

Key Words

Allah Muslim name for God

Arabic Middle Eastern language

calligraphy the art of handwriting

Eid al-Fitr festival to celebrate the end of Ramadan

halal food that Muslims are allowed to eat

haram food that Muslims are not allowed to eat

henna paste made from a henna plant that stains skin

hijab Muslim scarf or veil, worn by women

imam the man who leads prayers in a mosque

Islam the religion begun by Muhammad

minaret small tower on a mosque

mosque Muslim place of worship

Muslim person who follows the religion of Islam

pilgrimage journey to a holy place

prophets people chosen by Allah to spread his message

Qur'an Muslim holy book

Ramadan ninth month of the Muslim calendar, considered a holy month

salat Muslim prayers

Ummah worldwide community of Muslims

wudu special washing before prayers

Index

Log on to www.av2books.com

AV² by Weigl brings you media enhanced books that support active learning. Go to www.av2books.com, and enter the special code found on page 2 of this book. You will gain access to enriched and enhanced content that supplements and complements this book. Content includes video, audio, weblinks, quizzes, a slide show, and activities.

AV² Online Navigation

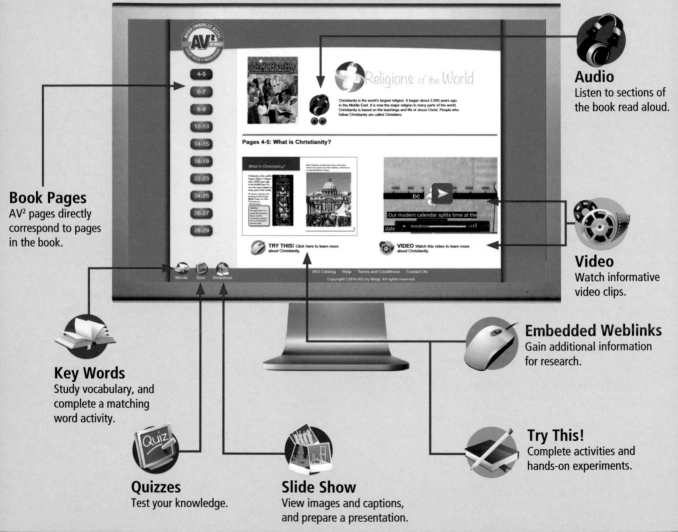

Book Pages
AV² pages directly correspond to pages in the book.

Audio
Listen to sections of the book read aloud.

Video
Watch informative video clips.

Key Words
Study vocabulary, and complete a matching word activity.

Embedded Weblinks
Gain additional information for research.

Quizzes
Test your knowledge.

Slide Show
View images and captions, and prepare a presentation.

Try This!
Complete activities and hands-on experiments.

AV² was built to bridge the gap between print and digital. We encourage you to tell us what you like and what you want to see in the future.

Sign up to be an AV² Ambassador at www.av2books.com/ambassador.